Food from Farmers

MEAT!

Life on a Sheep Farm

by Ruth Owen

WINDMILL
BOOKS ™

New York

Published in 2012 by Windmill Books, an Imprint of Rosen Publishing
29 East 21st Street, New York, NY 10010

Editor for Ruby Tuesday Books Ltd: Mark J. Sachner
U.S. Editor: Julia Quinlan
Designer: Emma Randall
Consultant: Logan Peterman, Laughing Sprout Family Farm

Photo Credits: Cover, 1, 4–5, 6–7, 8–9, 10–11, 12–13, 14 (top), 15, 16–17, 18–19, 20–21, 22–23, 24, 25 (center), 25 (bottom), 26–27, 28–29, 30 © Shutterstock; 14 (bottom) © FLPA; 25 (top) © Wikipedia Creative Commons (public domain).

Library of Congress Cataloging-in-Publication Data

Owen, Ruth, 1967–
 Meat! : life on a sheep farm / by Ruth Owen.
     p. cm. — (Food from farmers)
 Includes index.
 ISBN 978-1-61533-533-6 (library binding) — ISBN 978-1-61533-542-8 (pbk.) —
ISBN 978-1-61533-543-5 (6-pack)
 1. Sheep—Juvenile literature. 2. Sheep ranches—Juvenile literature. I. Title.
 SF375.2.O94 2012
 636.3—dc23
                              2011028925

Manufactured in the United States of America

CPSIA Compliance Information: Batch #BOW2102WM: For Further Information contact Windmill Books, New York, New York at 1-866-478-0556

CONTENTS

WELCOME TO MY FARM!

Hi! My name is Leon. I am nearly 12 years old. I live on a farm with my parents and my baby sister, Lisa. We raise sheep on our farm.

Hundreds of sheep live on our farm.
The number is always changing, though.
In the spring the lambs are born.
Then we may have around a thousand animals to care for!

Our sheep give us two products to sell, meat and wool.

Sheep's wool

Eddie

This is Eddie, one of our rams.
A ram is a male sheep.

Eddie is always trying to butt me, so I never
turn my back on him!

EDDIE'S SHEEP FARM FACTS

• There are over six million sheep in North America!

LET'S LOOK AROUND THE FARM

This is a map of our farm. We live in the farmhouse.

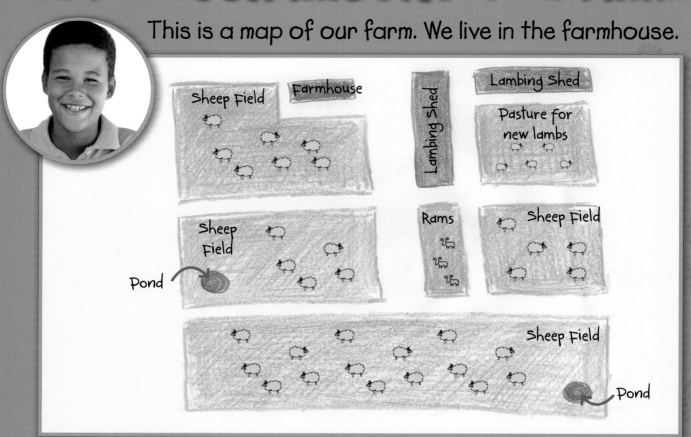

Sheep Field

Farmhouse

Lambing Shed

Lambing Shed

Pasture for new lambs

Sheep Field

Pond

Rams

Sheep Field

Sheep Field

Pond

The sheep live out in the fields most of the year.

Sheep and lambs are sometimes attacked by **predators** such as dogs, foxes, wolves, or coyotes.

One way we protect the sheep is by having electric fences. If a predator touches the fence, it gets an electric shock!

Rossi

We also have Lawrence and Rossi. They are our guard llamas.

Male llamas are good at keeping watch for predators. If a predator comes into the fields, they chase it away.

Lawrence

EDDIE'S SHEEP FARM FACTS

- Many farmers use guard llamas to protect animals such as sheep or chickens. A guard llama will kick a predator if it tries to attack!

7

MEET THE SHEEP!

Sheep live in groups called flocks.
Sheep are naturally a **prey** animal.
This means predators try to eat them.
So, sheep stick close together at all times.
Living in a flock gives the sheep lots of pairs
of eyes and ears to watch and listen for danger!

Flock

An adult female sheep is called a ewe. Because we **breed** sheep, most of the sheep on our farm are ewes.

Ewe

Lamb

Eddie, George, and Buster are our rams.
They are the fathers of all the lambs that we breed.

Eddie

George

Buster

In the fall, it's time for the ewes to **mate**.
Each ram is put in a field with a big group of ewes.
It's the ram's job to mate with all the females.

EDDIE'S SHEEP FACTS

- **A sheep that is under one year old is called a lamb.
Once it is over a year old, it is called a ewe or a ram.**

MEET THE TEAM!

If you take care of sheep, you are known as a shepherd. Our farm has two shepherds, Dad and Greg.

Dad

My baby sister, Lisa

Ruben

There are two other important team members. These are our herding dogs, Ruby and her son Ruben. Ruby and Ruben are Border collies.

Ruby

- **Border collies were first bred in an area on the border between England and Scotland.**

Border collies are smart and hardworking. They enjoy managing sheep and pleasing their owners.

When the sheep need to move fields, Ruby and Ruben herd them.
They also round up the sheep and herd them into the barn.
Dad and Greg use command words to tell the dogs what to do.

Greg

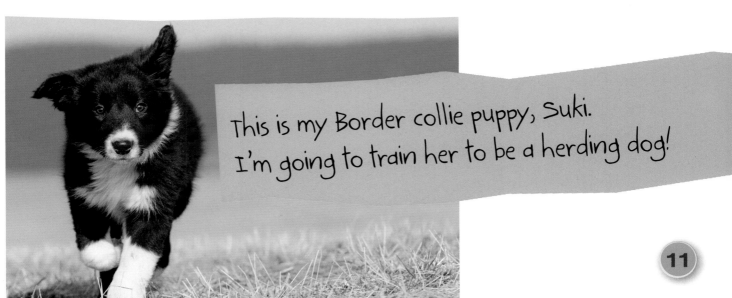

This is my Border collie puppy, Suki.
I'm going to train her to be a herding dog!

WHAT DO SHEEP EAT?

Sheep graze, or eat, grass and **pasture** plants such as clover.

Sheep also eat **weeds** and even poisonous plants that make other grazing animals sick.

These woolly, eating machines can be very useful!
Sheep are used to clear weeds in national parks and forests.

This sheep is eating weeds in a vineyard where wine grapes are grown.

Sheep are sometimes used to help stop wild fires. A herd of sheep will eat up a wide strip of grass and plants between houses and an area where a fire may start. If a wild fire reaches the empty strip, it cannot spread to the houses.

sheep feed

When our ewes are pregnant, we give them feed that includes corn, wheat, or oats. It also contains special **nutrients** to keep the ewes healthy.

EDDIE'S SHEEP FACTS

• A sheep grazes for around seven hours every day!

LAMBING TIME

Spring is the busiest time of year on our farm. This is when the lambs are born.

When it gets close to lambing time, the ewes are put in the lambing sheds.

Lambing shed

The ewes hang out in big pens and wait to give birth. While they wait, they eat dried grass called hay.

The ewes can give birth at any time, day or night. Dad, Mom, and Greg take turns watching over the ewes.

A ewe gives birth to one, two, or three lambs. The newborn lambs look a bit slimy, but the sheep moms soon lick them clean!

A newborn lamb can stand up after about 30 minutes.

Now, it can have its first drink of milk from its mother.

EDDIE'S SHEEP FARM FACTS

• Over 3.5 million lambs are born each year in the United States.

CARING FOR THE LAMBS

For the first few days, each ewe is put in a small pen with her lambs. This helps the family get to know each other. It also lets the lambs drink their mother's milk.

For the first few weeks of its life, a lamb drinks milk every hour.

After a few days, each sheep family is put in a big pen with other families.

When the lambs are two weeks old, we give them lamb feed made from corn and soybeans.
The lambs eat their feed in a pen called a creep feed.
Only the lambs are small enough to creep into this pen.
This stops the moms from stealing the tasty food!

EDDIE'S SHEEP FARM FACTS

• There are 914 different types of sheep in the world. In the U.S. 35 different types are raised.

LIFE AS A LAMB

When the spring weather gets warm, the sheep families go out into the fields.

The lambs watch their moms and learn how to graze.

EDDIE'S SHEEP FACTS

• A lamb can recognize its mom's bleat, or call, among hundreds of other sheep.

Lambs like to play!
They chase each other and jump on their moms' backs. Their favorite game is "king of the hill"!

King of the hill ⟶

When the lambs are around four months old, they are **weaned**. They are put in a separate field from their moms so they cannot drink milk. Now they get all their food from grazing.

We keep some of the female lambs on our farm. They will have lambs of their own next year.

The rest of the lambs will be sold for meat.

19

THE AUCTION SALE

We make money on our farm by selling our lambs for meat.

EDDIE'S MEAT FACTS

- Meat that comes from an animal under one year old is called "lamb." Meat from older sheep is called "mutton."

We sell some of our lambs at auction sales. Dad takes the lambs to the sale in the truck.

Sheep for sale

Cattle for sale

The person running the auction sale is called the auctioneer.

The auctioneer says a starting price for our lambs.
Then different buyers bid against each other.
It works like this. One buyer may agree to pay two hundred dollars. Another will then say, "Two hundred and twenty."
The bidding goes up and up until only one buyer is left.
That buyer has won the auction and bought our lambs!

Meat for sale in a supermarket

The buyers at an auction sale may be from a supermarket or a meat processing company.

MEAT FOR SALE!

We also sell our lambs' meat at local markets. The meat is prepared at a **processing plant** called an abattoir.

Dad takes the lambs to the abattoir. The workers at the abattoir give the lambs a small electric shock. This knocks them out so they suffer as little as possible.

Then, the butchers at the plant process their meat.

EDDIE'S MEAT FACTS

- Popular cuts of lambs' meat include lamb chops, rack of lamb, leg of lamb, and shoulder of lamb. The meat can be made into sausages and pies, too.

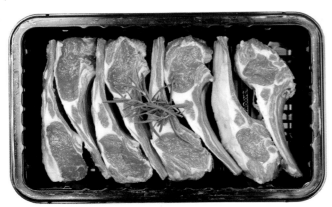

Lamb chops ↰

Rack of lamb

We take our lamb products to a local farmers' market. Here, farmers sell the things they have made or grown. You can buy fruit, vegetables, cheese, bread, and meat.

WONDERFUL WOOL!

In late spring, the sheep **shearers** come to our farm.

The shearers use electric clippers. They remove the sheep's fleece in one big piece. A shearer can shear a sheep in just two minutes!

Shearer

Clippers

Fleece

The fleeces are sold to a wool-processing plant. The fleeces are washed in soapy water to remove grease, called lanolin. Washing also removes grass, twigs, dirt, and sheep droppings!

EDDIE'S WOOL FACTS

• The oily lanolin from a fleece is separated from the washing water. It is used in products such as make-up and soap.

The wool is straightened on wire rollers.

Then the short pieces of straight wool are spun. This means they are tightly twisted together to create yarn.

Large machines spin the wool at the plant. People spin small quantities of wool using a spinning wheel.

Yarn

Wool

Spinning wheel

Now the yarn can be used for knitting or **weaving** cloth.

Dyed yarn

A DAY IN THE LIFE OF A FARM

During lambing time, Mom and Dad work almost non-stop!

Midnight
Dad keeps watch over five ewes that are all giving birth at the same time!

3:00 a.m.
Another two ewes give birth. Dad checks to see that the lambs are healthy.

7:00 a.m.
Dad and Mom give the ewes hay.

9:00 a.m.
Dad cleans out the pens and gives all the animals fresh straw bedding.

12:00 p.m.
One of the ewes dies giving birth.
Mom takes the orphan lamb into the farmhouse.
She must feed the lamb with bottles of milk.

3:00 p.m.
Greg starts work and Dad gets a nap!

5:00 p.m.
Mom, Dad, and Greg give the ewes water and more hay.

7:00 p.m.
Grandma comes over
to cook supper.

Time to give the orphan lamb another bottle of milk.

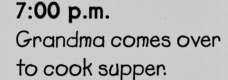

EDDIE'S SHEEP FARM FACTS

• **There are around 81,000 sheep farms in the United States.**

WE LOVE MEAT!

Meat tastes great, and it's very good for our bodies, too.

Meat contains **protein**. This is important for building strong bones and muscles. It keeps them healthy, too.

Of course, my favorite meat is lamb! Lamb contains **iron** and B **vitamins** that give you energy. It also contains **zinc**. Zinc is good for keeping your hair healthy and shiny.

These are *my* favorite ways to eat lamb.

Barbecue shish kebab

Lamb meatballs in spicy tomato sauce

Leg of lamb with roasted potatoes

Thank you to sheep farmers and sheep everywhere!

EDDIE'S SHEEP FARM FACTS

- **Some farms raise ewes for milking! Sheeps' milk is sold for drinking. It is also made into yogurt, ice cream, and cheeses, such as feta cheese.**

GLOSSARY

breed (BREED)
Put a male and female animal together so that they produce young.

iron (Y-urn)
A nutrient found in meat that is needed by your body. Your blood needs iron to help it carry oxygen around your body.

mate (MAYT)
When a male and female animal get together to produce young.

nutrients (Noo-tree-ents)
Substances that the body needs to help it live and grow. Foods contain nutrients such as vitamins and protein.

orphan (OR-fuhn)
An animal or person who has lost his or her parents. An animal that does not live with its father is considered an orphan when the mother dies.

pasture (PAS-chur)
A field where livestock, such as cows or sheep, can eat grass.

predator (PREH-duh-ter)
An animal that hunts and kills other animals for food.

prey (PRAY)
An animal that is hunted by another animal as food.

processing plant (PRAH-ses-ing PLANT)
A place, like a factory, where a series of actions are carried out to prepare or change something.

protein (PROH-teen)
A nutrient needed by the body. It is found in foods such as meat, fish, eggs, and milk.

shearer (SHEER-er)
A person who shears sheep, and sometimes llamas or alpacas, as their job. Shearers travel from farm to farm to shear flocks of sheep.

vitamin (VY-tuh-min)
A substance found in foods that is needed by the body for health and growth.

weaned (WEEND)
When an animal or young human no longer drinks milk but gets the nutrients it needs from solid foods.

weaving (WEEV-ing)
The threading together of yarns to make fabric. Weaving is done on a machine called a loom.

weed (WEED)
A plant growing where it is not wanted. Weeds are often tough, wild plants that grow very quickly.

zinc (ZINGK)
A nutrient that helps our bodies heal wounds and rebuild themselves. It is found in foods such as meat, shellfish, milk, and bread.

WEB SITES
For Web resources related to the subject of this book, go to: www.windmillbooks.com/weblinks and select this book's title.

READ MORE

Schaefer, Lola M. *Meat and Protein. Food Groups.* Chicago: Heinemann-Raintree, 2007.

Hewitt, Sally. *Meat and Fish. Good for Me.* New York: PowerKids Press, 2008.

Miller, Heather. *My Sheep. My Farm.* Connecticut: Children's Press, 2000.

INDEX